Affirmations

For Little Brown Boys
&
Little Brown Girls

Dedications

First I would like to pay dedication to source, God, the Universe. Secondly, special thanks to my mother for your constant love, and support. And last but not least, special thanks to my king, closest family members & Friends. This book is a dedication to little brown boys and girls. The children are, our future.

To the brown child,

With, Love.

Contents

PART 1 ....
For Brown Fathers and Brown Mothers *4-5*
Quick Guide: Using the Affirmations within this book................*6-8*

PART 2 ....
    Daily Affirmations *10-28*
        Prayer Affirmations *29-37*
PART 3...
Affirmations for Little Brown Boys...*38-46*
Affirmations for Little Brown Girls...*47-56*

PART 4...
Why "Brown" instead of "Black"?..*57-59*

Part 1

For Brown Fathers & Brown Mothers

"If I had one wish it would be for all fathers and mothers to read to their little princes and princesses again".
~N. P. Thomas

For Brown Fathers and Brown Mothers

It seems as though reading to our children is now becoming a thing of the past, not for all of us but for some of us with the somewhat over demands of everyday life. Nowadays we would rather entertain ourselves with the pleasures of reading fictions, non-fictions and fantasies. Rather than cater to the needs of our children's imaginations, and developing minds, through sharing moments with them like our parents and/or grandparents may have with us through night-time stories.

Now, this is not to disregard the brown father, and mother, but to empower them with hopes of uniting the brown family at its core, through connecting the parents and the children through literature. Our children are, our future so let us give them something positive to fill their developing mind's with, and affirm to them that they can be anything that they desire to be, and that they most certainly can achieve all of their hopes and their dreams.

As do we benefit from affirmations within our daily lives, our young princes and princesses should learn the power of affirmation, so that they are equipped with a great tool to apply within every stage of their lives. I have a dream, for this book to be passed down to generations to come, with hope that each young, and developed mind that shares the magic of this book will experience self-knowing in the moment and moments to come. With love to the brown father and the brown mother, your role never goes unrecognized. X

Part 1

Quick Guide:
Using the affirmations within this book

Quick Guide: Using the Affirmations in this book

All of the affirmations within this book can be recited as many times as necessary and may be used at any point throughout the day, as a means to get your young prince and/or princess into the practice of self love from as early as possible, in order for them to be self loving, and self empowering to themselves throughout their life course.

Though it can be, this book does not have to be read following the traditional approach of book reading, which would be from beginning to end, as this is not a story book, but a self empowerment book, specifically for young brown boys and girls, with an aim of teaching them the power of self empowerment through a system of speaking positive-self-enabling words out loud and to themselves. Rather, this book can be used as a reference guide, where both you and your child, open up the book to any page, where the affirmation that may benefit your child will be revealed.

The author advises that affirmations are recited as frequently as possible, in order for your child to fully benefit from the power of repetition which will allow the subconscious, and conscious mind to work together in creating patters associated with the combination of repeated positive words and phrases.

The Author Recommends

Focus on one affirmation with your child for a period of 7 days (before moving onto another affirmation), encouraging them to recite the affirmation aloud with you or by themselves as much as they are possibly comfortable with. In turn, these acts of reputation will familiarize your child with the words, which will reinforce their acceptance and knowing towards these sets of words. *Genius, Right.*

E.g. Daily Affirmation: 'I can be anything that I desire to be, and I most certainly can achieve all of my hopes and my dreams', (Use affirmation for 7 days).

Some parents may like to write affirmations on the child's white boards in their room, so that the child can also make a visual connection to affirmations. Sparking a connection within their subconscious minds, thus forming a constant association with positive words about themselves.

Most of all, have fun with this book of affirmations, knowing that your child is learning how to self-empower and love themselves through the magic of affirmations.

I love myself x

Part 2

Daily Affirmations

You and your child can recite these affirmations as regular as possible in order to encourage self-esteem, and confidence.

It is encouraged to focus on 1-2 affirmations to recite weekly, as consistently as possible in order for these confirmations of self to be embedded into the child's subconscious mind. In turn, a consistent practice will engrain self-esteem as well as self-knowledge within your child.

Daily Affirmations

I can be anything that I desire to be, and I most certainly can achieve all of my hopes, and my dreams.

When I have a dream that I want to achieve I work at it everyday.

All I have to do is put my mind to something, and I will accomplish it.

I love myself, I love my life, I love my family, and I love the world.

I trust in myself
(x4).

Daily Affirmations

I am thankful for my life, and for my body.

I love myself for who I am
(x4).

I LOVE how I look when I look at myself in the mirror.

I smile and laugh daily because I am happy.

Daily Affirmations

I am a happy child (x4).

I have a happy life (x4).

I am smart (x4).

I am BRAVE (x4).

Daily Affirmations

I treat others in a kind way, because I like to be treated in a kind way.

I say nice things to my friends because they are my friends.

I am strong. I am brave. I am kind. I am AMAZING.

Daily Affirmations

The colour of my skin is beautiful.

The colour of my hair is fantastic.

The colour of my eyes are perfect.

I am unique, and I am wonderful.

Daily Affirmations

I love myself <u>UNCONDITIONALLY</u>. That means that I will always love myself.

My friends are unique, and my friends are wonderful.

I am brown and I am wonderful.

Daily Affirmations

I am loved so much by my parents.

I have a beautiful mind (x4).

I listen to my heart (x4).

I am intelligent (x4).

I am peaceful (x4).

Daily Affirmations

I love myself even when I fail at something.

I love myself because I am the best.

The universe protects me all the time.

Daily Affirmations

I am helpful to others and myself. I am helpful at home.

I work to the best of my ability when I am at school.

I have happy thoughts. I am happy thoughts, and happy thoughts are me.

Daily Affirmations

I get better and better every new day.

I get stronger and stronger every new day.

I get smarter and smarter every new day.

I get happier and happier every new day.

Daily Affirmations

I love the sun (x4). I love the moon (x4). I love myself (x4).

I love the world(x4) I love the Earth (x4) I love myself (x4).

I enjoy learning because it makes me smarter.

I believe in myself
(x5).

Daily Affirmations

I am ALWAYS honest with my mummy and daddy.

I am AWESOME, and nobody can tell me otherwise.

I am perfect just the way I am
(x4).

Daily Affirmations

I don't listen to people who tell me that I can't achieve my dreams, because I know that I CAN!

I am a nourished child, who thrives of loving energy.

I like to EAT foods that are good for me.

Daily Affirmations

I am healthy inside and outside.

I am thankful for my family.

I am a smart student in my class (daycare).

I am proud of myself and all that I do.

Daily Affirmations

I am thankful to be ME
(x4).

I am a WINNER in life
(x4).

I like myself
(x4).

Daily Affirmations

Wonderful things happen to me.

I am kind to everybody no matter what the colour of his or her skin is.

I am kind to myself, to my friends, to my sibling, to my cousins.

I never ever give up, because I CAN do anything.

I am a peaceful child.

Daily Affirmations

I tell the truth about I how I am feeling.

I always say how I am feeling.

I respect all living things no matter what they are.

I am a magnet who always attracts blessings into my life.

Daily Affirmations

I am kind to all living things, all animals, and all insects because they do not harm me.

I embrace all of my emotions. That means I love myself when I am happy, and I still love myself when I am sad.

I may cry when I fall down, and it may hurt, but after I hug myself and smile because I am strong.

I am here on earth for a reason. God chooses me.

I say nice things about myself and about others.

I know that I am no better than anyone else. We are all on different paths. We are all great in our own ways.

Part 2

<u>Prayer Affirmations</u>

Can be used as night-time and wake up prayers that children and parents recite together, or that child recites to parent.

Prayers with ** besides them are interactive prayers that can be recited with actions to represent things in the prayer.

Can also be used if non-religious.

Prayer Affirmations

** I am the sun, the moon and all that is (x3).
Amen

I love myself. I love my sibling (if any). I love my friends. I love my mummy. I love my daddy. I love my grandma. I love my granddad. I love my cousin. I love my uncle. I love my aunt. I love life.
Amen

** I go to sleep happy, and I wake up happy. I go to sleep peaceful, and I wake up peaceful. I go to sleep, and I love myself. I wake up, and I love myself.
Amen

I pray to the universe, to bless me everyday because I am a good child.
Amen

Prayer Affirmations

I am a blessed child. I am a lucky child. I am a smart child. I am a happy child.
Amen

** I am all that is. That means that I am as great as the moon, I shine as bright as the sun, and at night I twinkle with the stars. I am all that is and all that is, is I.
Amen

I am blessed, and the universe chooses me because I am blessed. I am blessed, and I love my family, and myself at all times. I am blessed. I am blessed. I am blessed, and I am the best me.
Amen

Prayer Affirmations

I pray for love. I pray for laughter. I pray for my mummy, and I pray for my daddy. I pray for my friends, and teachers too. Overall I pray to always be blessed by you.
Thank you God.
Amen

I pray for happiness. I pray for peace. I pray for kindness in the world. I pray for the animals, and the trees. I pray because I love all things, and all things love me.
Amen

Prayer Affirmations

** I am a blessed child. I am as strong as a lion, and as tall as a tree. I am a blessed child. I love the birds, the bees, and the fish in the sea. I am a blessed child, and the universe and God loves me.
Amen

I pray to say thank you for all that I have, and all that I am. I pray because I am happy. I pray because I am smart. I pray to say thank you. I pray for the universe, and god to always protect me.
Amen

I pray to say thank you for all that I have, and all that I am. I pray because I am happy. I pray because I am smart. I pray to say thank you. I pray for the universe, and god to always protect my family and I.
Amen

Prayer Affirmations

I pray to my higher self for peace, for love, for protection, for guidance, for happiness, for health, and for abundance.
Amen

** I am a child of the sun. I am a child of the moon. I am a child of the stars. I am a child of the universe. I am a child of God. That means I am a child that is blessed. I am a child that is protected, and most of all I am a child that is loved always and forever.
Amen

I am thankful for this beautiful day. I am thankful for this beautiful life. I am thankful for my healthy body. I am thankful for my healthy mind. I am thankful and always will be.
Amen

Prayer Affirmations

I pray for good health. I pray for good food to eat. I pray for those who have less than me. I pray for love, and happiness for everybody.
Amen

I woke up today, so I will just like to say, "God, I am happy to be alive, and I am a very thankful child".
Amen

I am thankful for my home. I am thankful for my school. I am thankful for my clothes, and I am thankful for my toys. I am thankful.
Amen

I pray when I rise, and I pray when I sleep for blessings and protection of everybody. I pray for the strong, and I pray for the weak. I pray when I rise, and I pray when I sleep. I pray for love, and I pray for harmony.
Amen

Prayer Affirmations

I pray for strength. I pray for the world. I pray for the animals. I pray to be happy.
Amen

Thank you for the air I breathe. Thank you for the food I eat. Thank you for my hands and feet. Thank you for making me complete.
Amen

Thank you for the day. Thank you for the night. Thank you for my mummy, and thank you for all of my family.
Amen

Prayer Affirmations

Thank you for the day. Thank you for the night. Thank you for my daddy, and thank you for all of my family.
Amen

I pray for the angels to watch over me. I pray for the angels to protect me. I pray for the angels to be with me everywhere that I go. I pray for the angels to hear me. I pray for the angels to be with me when I wake up. I pray for the angels to be with me when I close my eyes to fall asleep.
Amen

My mind is healthy. My heart is healthy. My spirit is healthy. I am healthy.
Amen

Part 3

Affirmations for little Brown Boys

This section can also be read by little brown girls in order for them to have a positive view toward the little brown boy, and the male figure overall. It is helpful for little brown girls to also speak positively toward the opposite sex in an empowering manner. Suggested for little brown girls who have brothers.

Affirmations for Little Brown Boys

I am a strong, intelligent, and wise young brown boy.

I am a respectful, and knowledgeable young brown prince.

I stand up for myself using my words, and the intelligence in my mind, not my fists.

I stand up for what is right, and not what is wrong because I am a strong, intelligent brown prince.

Affirmations for Little Brown Boys

I am a handsome young brown prince who will one day be a handsome brown king.

I may feel scared sometimes and that's okay but I always remember that I am a brown prince and I have courage.

I may fall down sometimes, but even when I do, I dust myself of and get back up because I am brave.

I go to school to learn, to work hard, and to pay attention because learning helps me to grow wiser.

Affirmations for Little Brown Boys

I go to school to learn, to work hard, and to pay attention because learning helps me to grow smarter.

I am a brown prince. My mummy is a brown queen. My daddy is a brown king. We are a strong, loving family.

I love the colour of my skin. The colour of my skin makes me handsome, and it makes me who I am.

I offer my friend a helping hand when they fall down. I ask them are they okay because I am a kind, and strong brown prince.

Affirmations for Little Brown Boys

I know who I am. I am a Son of God
(x4).

I can do anything because I am amazing inside and outside.

I love my hair. I love my handsome eyes. I love my handsome nose. I love my handsome lips. I love myself from the crown of my head all the way down to my toes.

I wear an invisible crown on my head at all times because I am a prince, and when I grow up I will be a king.

Affirmations for Little Brown Boys

I am a smart capable student. No matter what my grades look like, I will always make progress to achieve more.

I am a smart, capable student, and I am always proud of myself, and of my efforts.

I am handsome. I am intelligent. I am strong. I am healthy (x4).

I am a brown king, and I am a leader (x4).

Affirmations for Little Brown Boys

I always make my mummy and my daddy proud in all that I do
(x4).

I learn from my mistakes. I learn from challenges and I get better because of them.

I express myself at all times. If I like something, I say it. If I dislike something, I say it. If I am happy, I show it. If I am sad, I show it.

I am powerful. I am resilient
(x4).

I am as strong as a lion
(x4).

Affirmations for Little Brown Boys

I can do anything that I put my mind too. The words "I can't" are not in my vocabulary. I can do anything.

I CAN. I CAN. I CAN. I CAN!

I am productive and I am focused because I am an intelligent young man.

I am in control. Nobody can shake me. Nobody can cause me to be sad. Nobody can cause me to be angry. I am in control. I am at peace.

Affirmations for Little Brown Boys

I can achieve all that I want. EVERYTHING is possible.

I am BRAVE enough to become anything that I want to become.

I know that I am a blessed child. I am a blessed child (x4).

I am the master of my life. I am the king of my castle (x4).

I am destined for BIG things. I am destined for GREATNESS.

I Am Possible (x4).

Part 3

<u>Affirmations for Little Brown Girls</u>

This section is not exclusive to just the little brown girl, but can also be read by little brown boys in order for them to have a positive view toward the little brown girl & women overall. It is helpful for little brown boys to also speak positively toward the opposite sex in an empowering manner. Suggested for little brown boys who have sisters.

Affirmations for Little Brown Girls

I am a brown princess. I speak with love in my heart, and with kindness in my words.

I am a brown and beautiful girl (x4).

I love my beautiful hair. I love my beautiful eyes. I love my beautiful nose. I love my beautiful lips. I love myself from the crown of my head all the way down to my beautiful toes.

Affirmations for Little Brown Girls

I am a brown princess, and I have greatness inside of me
(x4)

I know who I am. I am a Daughter of God
(x4).

I always use my mind to do things that I really like to do because I have a strong and intelligent mind.

I am one of a kind, and I am a beautiful girl
(x4).

Affirmations for Little Brown Girls

I love myself. I love my brownness. I love that I am beautiful. I love that I am smart. I love the magic within my heart.

I am uniquely gifted. Nobody in the world can be me. I am the only girl who is amazing at being me.

I radiate love. I radiate joy. I radiate happiness. I radiate golden energy because I shine as bright as the sun.

I am Enough! Just the way I am!
(x4).

Affirmations for Little Brown Girls

I deserve to be happy and free because I am a free spirit
(x4).

I am a healthy, intelligent, wise, and kind brown girl
(x4).

My skin is a beautiful shade of brown and I sparkle like gold
(x4).

I am a generous, openhearted, wise young princess
(x4).

Affirmations for Little Brown Girls

My mind is healthy. My heart is healthy. My spirit is healthy. My body is healthy (x4).

I am a beautiful brown princess and one day I will be a beautiful brown queen like my mummy.

I am thankful because I am COMPLETE. I am completely smart. I am completely kind. I am completely capable. I am completely beautiful.

Affirmations for Little Brown Girls

My hair is perfect. My hair is my princess crown. My hair is strong. My hair is soft. My hair is beautiful. I love my hair.

I express myself about how I feel to other people because I have a right to express myself.

I have greatness that lives within me, because I am destined for greatness.

Affirmations for Little Brown Girls

I am always proud of myself, and the princess that I am.

I am always proud of myself. I am becoming a wonderful young woman.

I am happy to be me because I am an amazing, strong girl!

I surround myself with love and light because I am a princess.

Affirmations for Little Brown Girls

I am a princess, so I bring peace, happiness and joy to myself and to others.

I always smile, even when I am feeling sad, because my smile is like the sun. It lights up the whole world.

I do not need the approval of others because I approve of myself. That's what princesses do.

I AM good enough. I have enough, and I am enough!

I give myself permission to SHINE as bright as the sun does.

I am positive (x4).

I am Beautiful (x4).

Part 4

Why "Brown" instead of "Black"?

Does it really matter?

The author of this book respects and acknowledges the fact that as 'black' people, we are a blessed people that come with many different, and unique shades of our tone of skin. The author chooses to use the word brown, instead of the word black, as brown includes and embraces every shade of the pigment that there is across the spectrum. From darker toned skin, to lighter toned skin.

The author wants to include all brown skinned children, who may also be of mixed nationalities, apart of the brown race. This is a book that embraces all brown skinned children whether darker, or lighter toned, from Africa, or mixed with brown, and another race. Brown is Brown.

After all, black is a colour more representational of the colour of the ink used within the pages of this book more so than a skin tone. There are lighter, and darker variations of the colour brown, as opposed to the colour black, which does not have more than one variation.

Think outside of the box, and encourage your children to do so as well.

Affirmation: *'Life is AMAZING'*

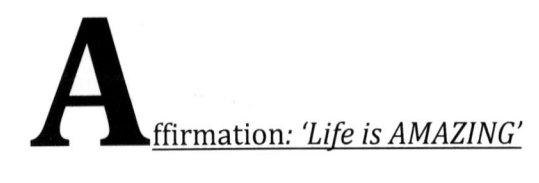

The End

Thank you for reading.

~N. P. Thomas

Printed in Great Britain
by Amazon